T0194652

TENDER WHISPERS OF LOVE: POETRY

SOOTHING WORDS FOR THE REAL WORLD

ELLEN RICHARDSON

WESTBOW
PRESS®
A DIVISION OF THOMAS NELSON
& ZONDERVAN

WestBow Press books may be ordered through booksellers or by contacting:

WestBow Press
A Division of Thomas Nelson & Zondervan
1663 Liberty Drive
Bloomington, IN 47403
www.westbowpress.com
1 (866) 928-1240

ISBN: 978-1-9736-6640-0 (sc)
ISBN: 978-1-9736-6641-7 (hc)
ISBN: 978-1-9736-6639-4 (e)

Library of Congress Control Number: 2019907994

Print information available on the last page.

WestBow Press rev. date: 11/8/2019

This book is dedicated to those who are war-weary and heaven-bent.

CONTENTS

Part III. On Hope in Jesus

On Appreciation

I owe Teerat Jackree and Kathleen Sutcliffe each an enormous debt of gratitude; without them, there would be no book.

I thank my late father for the marvelous and most precious memories, for my mother, and my sister in particular, for helping me build a home post-injury. I also thank my dear sister and my lawyer, David McGhee for their work on the lawsuit.

Lastly and mostly, I thank God the Father; Jesus, His Son, and the Holy Spirit, who truly work all things for good (Romans 8:28).

INTRODUCTION

Kathy Troccoli sings, "Life can be so good and life can be so hard."

Though we sometimes don't like to think about it, the world we live in is troubled. Sometimes it seems like so much is coming at us at once, and we don't know what to do or where to turn. Maybe you can relate. Certainly that was how I felt while growing up.

I was raised by a single mother, and there was much havoc in my little world. In hindsight, a deep darkness of fear, anxiety, worry, and depression surrounded me.

When I was twenty-three in 1987, Jesus wooed me as is His way: so many monarch butterflies flew in my line of vision that summer that I started to think Someone was trying to get my attention.

Not knowing about the butterflies, a friend then invited me to her church, which happened to be world-renowned; there, because of my newfound belief in the existence of God, and because a faithful pastor gave an altar call, I accepted Jesus's forgiveness for my sins, making Him Lord of my life. Things have never been the same since.

Around the time of my conversion, I was also diagnosed with a biochemical disease of the brain called depression, or major depressive disorder, an illness that has no known cure but is treatable with medication.

After spending years coming to grips with my need for the meds, I gained stability, and my disease went into remission, so much so that I was able to complete two degrees, a BRE, and an MDiv in Counselling, graduating in 1998.

The major premise of this book is that just as we had no say in how we came into the world, we are to have no say in how we leave it, that all suffering has meaning in the eternal realm. Now you may think that you cannot relate to this, that life is currently great. But I will say that you don't know what a day can bring. Sometimes, we need to invest some time to fortify ourselves, to brace and prepare for a future where anything can happen. Certainly, I did not bank on this paralysis of mine. It came as an utter shock at the time. The aforementioned major premise comes from someone who's been there.

You see, because of this biochemical disease of the brain, I'm sad to report that I tried to end my life on three separate occasions, all serious attempts. Hallelujah, despite my intentions, Jesus spared my life, possibly to speak into your difficult life today. In fact, with one of those attempts, my family pursued a lawsuit; I'm happy to say that we won! It deemed that certain psychiatrists were responsible for a jump from a bridge known for its lethality. That attempt landed me in a wheelchair with paraplegia.

I learned the hard way (isn't it often the case?) that suicide, whether by one's own hand or assisted by a physician, is not an option. There is healing and hope for all who choose to earnestly seek it. God says in the Bible that He will be found when you seek Him with all of your heart (Jeremiah 29:13). You too can find joy and love even in the midst of the most agonizing of circumstances.

I wrote the rough draft of the majority of this book while living in an institution following rehab for my spinal cord injury. Thankfully, I got out of that place only to be dubbed, *Ellen of Joy* by a friend a year and a half later.

Eight years went by, and one day out of the blue, while I was visiting him, my father approached me and asked me about this God I knew. I was shocked! All my life, I had known my father to have a love of money, and here he was in his seventy-ninth year inquiring about Jesus! There and then, he came to know Jesus as his personal Savior, receiving His forgiveness. I was elated! It was a very special time for me indeed.

Three years later, my dad told me I was teaching him how to love. He was among the over seventy individuals whom I have had the privilege of helping to seal a personal relationship with Jesus to date.

I've learned joy and love not from my family or from a spouse but from Jesus, my Lord. I've actually had spans of years when I did not have any close relative or friend, only Jesus. He is enough. Don't get me wrong; I did have friends. Just no one following me closely.

This book has a companion, called *Tender Whispers of Love*. It is a book of prose whose rough draft was also written while I lived in the institution. It has the same major premise. They both offer a proven way of life that, if applied, will have you learning with Paul "to be content whatever the circumstances" (Philippians 4:11).

Ellen Richardson
October 2019

PART I

ON EMOTIONS

ETERNAL LOVE

"God is love,"* pure love
Of an eternal kind.
Not love as we know it,
But unique, you will find.

For sometimes what He allows
And what He does†
Causes great pain,
Doesn't look anything like love.

He uses it to mold you,
To draw you to Him.
He bids you surrender
And let Him deeply in.

He doesn't stop calling
Till your life is through.
He weighs all you are
And all that you do.‡

For He wants you to know
Him more deeply, Him more,
So you can relate to Him better
When you get to that heavenly shore.

---

* 1 John 4:16.

† "'For my thoughts are not your thoughts, neither are your ways my ways,' declares the Lord" (Isa. 55:8).

‡ "[Jesus] will reward each person according to what they have done" (Matt. 16:27b); "[T]he Lord will reward each one for whatever good they do" (Eph. 6:8); "[P]eople are destined to die once, and after that to face judgment" (Heb. 9:27).

A Heart Full of Love

Open your heart up to His,
And you will find there
A heart full of love
To hold your every care.

Open your heart,
And you will see
That He'll give and teach love
Oh so tenderly.

He, by His very nature,
Is love, pure love.
Nothing can replace
What comes from above.

For He can bestow
On anyone and everyone
This fruit of the Spirit.*
He asks you just to come.

To receive His Spirit
Is the very first step.
He crumbles a heart of stone.**

He replaces it
With a heart overflowing,
With a soft one all His own.

A fleshy heart
He will give.
He will help you
To really live

And love in ways divine.
Oh, mold me and take me.
Make me wholly Thine.

---

*"But the fruit of the Spirit is love, joy, peace, forbearance, kindness, goodness, faithfulness, gentleness and self-control. Against such things there is no law" (Gal. 5:22–23).

** "I will give them an undivided heart and put a new spirit in them; I will remove from them their heart of stone and give them a heart of flesh. Then they will follow my decrees and be careful to keep my laws. They will be my people, and I will be their God" (Ezek. 11:19–20).

Alone and Cold

Alone and cold—
That's how I feel.

I remember at four,
Standing and watching
Violence in our home.

That feeling,
That alone and cold,

Resonates in my being.
It stays with me
And comes up
Again and again.

There is Your promise
To never leave nor forsake.*
But I don't feel You,
For goodness' sake!

Your Presence eludes.
My pain it exudes,
Seems from each and every pore.

And I feel all alone.
Don't have a home.
Feel afraid at my very core.

But trust You I must.
Must take that leap
And trust in Your Word.

For though I may not feel it,
I'm really never alone.
In my spirit, Jesus be heard.

---

* The Lord Himself commissions Joshua after the death of Moses, saying:

> As I was with Moses, so I will be with you; I will never leave you nor forsake you. Be strong and courageous, because you will lead these people to inherit the land I swore to their ancestors to give them.
>
> Be strong and very courageous. Be careful to obey all the law my servant Moses gave you; do not turn from it to the right or to the left, that you may be successful wherever you go.
>
> Do not let this Book of the Law depart from your mouth; meditate on it day and night, so that you may be careful to do everything written in it. Then you will be prosperous and successful.

Have I not commanded you? Be strong and courageous. Do not be terrified; do not be discouraged, for the Lord your God will be with you wherever you go (Josh. 1:5–9).

COME OUT AND BE STRONG

Living on the edge,
The edge of despair.
Climb out of the hole,
Only to fall back there.

I gain some ground,
Then something happens
To plunge me back down deep

To where I struggle,
To where I hide
Myself, my dreams out of reach.

Where I go to hide
From the dust and the din,
Can't feel Him near,
Won't let Him in.

This is familiar;
I know this place.
This was my home;
Spent years in this space.

But do I, do you, when you
Spend extended time here,

Stomp on His grace
Instead of to Jesus drawing near?

We all have bad days.
He knows and understands.
But try to remember what it's doing
To Him and all your fans.

Dampen their spirits you do
When you choose to live in a shoe.
Come out and be strong.
You know, it hasn't all gone wrong.

FEAR

I get in touch with my feelings,
Only to see me going under again.
I get in touch with my feelings,
Only to want to run and then.

Fear threatens to grip me
And have me in its vice.
I say, Okay, I'm fearful again.
I need some good advice.

So I go to God.
I cry and cry out.
He listens, He advises.

He encourages and lifts.
My honesty He loves.
My sin He despises.

"Be still and know
That I am God."*
I sit with Him, my Friend.

As He guides me in prayer,
He leads me to safety.
My wounded heart He does mend.

"Oh, free me," I plead.
"Release me from fear's grip
So I do not go reeling
On another trip

Designed by Satan
To pull me away
From You and Your grace,
And cause me to stray."

"We all, like sheep, have gone astray,
each of us has turned to our own way."†
Your Word—it comforts when I do give in.
For each and every one of us is so very precious to Him.

Alert me, Lord, when fear threatens to engulf.
Catch me from succumbing to Satan's tool.
Teach me that You are faithful.
Help me to trust You in Your school.

---

* Psalm 46:10.

† Isaiah 53:6a.

THE ETERNAL METHOD

God uses ways*
That are all His own.
The Eternal Method
Makes me groan.

Groan "Why?"
or "How could you?"
All the while,
He knows what to do

To make me rich,
To make me stand firm,
To give me hope
So I won't squirm

Out of my responsibilities
To Him and to others.
He gave me His Book,
And my sisters and brothers.

Sometimes, though, I don't get it.
His eternal method
He does use.

His Way of teaching:
He puts me through things
That me they downright confuse!

Still, a mustard seed faith†
Is all that He needs
To grow me up and make …

… make me rich
In my spirit.
He gives, but beware—He also can take.‡

---

* "'For my thoughts are not your thoughts, neither are your ways my ways,' declares the Lord" (Isa. 55:8).

† "Truly I tell you, if you have faith as small as a mustard seed, you can say to this mountain, 'Move from here to there' and it will move" (Matt. 17:20).

‡ "The Lord gave and the Lord has taken away; may the name of the Lord be praised" (Job 1:21).

A DYNAMIC RELATIONSHIP*

In relationship I am
With the Great I Am.
Sometimes it's hard
To make sense of You,

For You do things
I just don't get it.
They're unfathomable, eternal.
Sometimes I just want to quit.

It's a dynamic relationship,
A moving toward and a moving away.
And this back-and-forth
Can change from day to day.

Sometimes I'm
Inexplicably in love,
Praising You, my Savior,
Gratefully gazing above.

Sometimes I feel thrown,
Even have disdain,
Because You show me things
That cause me great pain.

But in the end,
You have my freedom in mind.
My suffering is for my benefit—
Benefit of an eternal kind.

_____

*Written soon after I had my spinal cord injury.

DRUNK WITH GRIEF

I am drunk with grief,
Drunk with despair.
Social mores—
I don't even care.

Singing loudly and long
In the open sanctuary
When no one is there,

I shout to the crucifix
On the wall, "Curse you!"
In full humanity, I do even dare,

For I'm angry and bitter,*
Bitter as can be.
My blood boils over;
It rages deep inside of me.

This horror in my life
Is more than I can take!
You know that and You use it.
With it, You want to make…

… make my character richer and deeper,
But You won't counter my free will.
You hope I'll reach out, not turn away.
You hope I'll reach to You still.

You say, "Trust Me, not your feelings!"
Little by little, step by step, you're healing.
You guide me through the muck and the mire.
Creating inner beauty is what You desire.

Right now, I don't want to hear it.
But I know You are the Way.**
If I don't trust You with this,
In the end, I'm gonna pay...

... pay with prolonged grief
And agony for sure.
Trusting Your strength in me
Is the only true cure

To my hopelessness,
To the anger, the bitterness.
Trusting in You to guide me through.
Please give me the patience

To endure the process. Oh, let there come a time
When I'll be able to say,
"I've learned a lot, it makes some sense,"†
And then live for Judgment Day.

---

* Written near the onset of my physical disability. Good counseling and time helped heal here. "For lack of guidance a nation falls, but victory is won through many advisers (Prov. 11:14). "Surely you need guidance to wage war, and victory is won through many advisers" (Prov.

24:6). "The way of fools seems right to them, but the wise listen to advice" (Prov.12:15).

** "Jesus answered, 'I am the way and the truth and the life. No one comes to the Father except through me'" (John 14:6).

† Though I never have known why God allowed those particular forms of suffering—the biochemical mental sickness, and the paralysis in my life—still some years after writing this poem, I could honestly say that upon looking back on all God had led me through, I was grateful for the suffering expressed here because I had witnessed and learned firsthand about suffering in the world on a level of which I had never before been exposed, and, as well, been witness to God's faithfulness through it all.

A Selfish God?

What a God
But a selfish one
Would take most of my life,
Then ask me to go on?

He didn't save me, it seems,
Or provide a way out
When all that was within me
Was bitter rage and doubt.

The bitter rage persisted,
Was as strong as it could be.
Anger so vile,
Deep inside of me.

Anger for them,
And for myself too,
Could not escape
The self-loathing for true.

Satan gets us down
And wants us to stay
In despair so long.

He plants in our hearts
Seeds of destruction
That can feel so very strong.

With grief of any kind,
Waves recurring and relentless
Toward our feelings,
We can feel so defenseless.

But just know that
Satan is a defeated foe.
God can forge,
Out of deep despair, hope.

For a human spirit
Is resilient for true.
God is really there
For me and for you.

To take what's so precious
And ask me to go on
Seems to me selfish, though.
Or could I be wrong?

What kind of love
Is that which requires
A stripping of what
One hopes or desires?

A revamping of life.
A restructuring too.
Hopes and dreams revisited.
He makes everything new.*

Can I possibly say
That He knows what He's doing?
Can I really just trust?

One sweet day,
He'll make all things clear.
Cling to the hope of that day† I must.

---

* "He who was seated on the throne said, 'I am making everything new!'" (Rev. 21:5)

† "[P]eople are destined to die once, and after that to face judgment" (Heb. 9:27).

BITTERNESS

It threatens to take you.
It threatens to make you:
Unforgiving, unyielding, hating, biting.

It keeps you from you.
It keeps you from me too.
It keeps you from wrongs righting.

Hate, hate.
It cries,
Destroy,
Despise.

It threatens to take your soul.
It'll swallow you whole.
It wants to engulf you.
It is Satan's strong tool.

It is a great foe,
For it wants your soul to fare
Not the body but the soul
Into a living nightmare,

Where it blocks out
That which is good,
For it goes on a mission.
Destroy and destroy it could.

Destroy relationships,
Friends, relatives, loved ones.
Get out the knives,
The bullets, the guns.

Destroy even yourself.
It won't stop at anything.
It'll make you its slave.
It'll take your wedding ring.

It eats away at all that's dear.
It'll spread far those that are near.
Beware, I say, beware.
To dance extended with it,* don't dare.

It's part of deep grieving, though.†
So if you feel it, let it come,
But know it must pass.
Into its grasp, you dare not succumb.

Let this be a warning, then,
To you and all you hold dear.
Don't hold on to bitterness,‡
But to Jesus draw very near.

---

* "See to it that no one falls short of the grace of God and that no bitter root grows up to cause trouble and defile many" (Heb. 12:15).

† "Each heart knows its own bitterness, and no one else can share its joy" (Prov. 14:10).

‡ "And do not grieve the Holy Spirit of God, with whom you were sealed for the day of redemption. Get rid of all bitterness, rage and anger, brawling and slander, along with every form of malice. Be kind and compassionate to one another, forgiving each other, just as in Christ God forgave you" (Eph. 4:30–32).

VULNERABILITY

No one should be paralyzed
With this world being as it is,
Fraught with anguish and pain.

They say, "Life is difficult,"
Even without this grief.
Now it's doubly so and again.

"Life is complicated."
"Life is unfair."
The devil, he calls me
To live it in despair.

A fight I'm called to,
And fight I will do.
God's trained my hands for war.*

I won't give in
To Satan
And blame God for this deep horror.

I know He's got a plan
For me and for you.
He has broken me
For a purpose too.

Does my vulnerable state remind
You of your own brokenness inside?
You know, that part of you
You always try to hide?

Could it be? Is God pointing out
With my own fragility?
Is He trying to help you see
Your own real, deep, human vulnerability?

---

* "Praise be to the LORD my Rock, who trains my hands for war, my fingers for battle" (Ps. 144:1).

A Feeling of Power

There is a feeling of power
That I received as a youngster,
Growing up in the home I did.

My Mom asked me to be
Caretaker, counselor,
And in those roles I hid.

Wow! To be smart enough
And brave enough too.
To instruct my own mother
And tell her what to do!

Gave me an awesome sense
Of power, of "maturity."
Gave me the illusion
That I was in control.

Gave me a feeling too
That I could do anything,
If I could to my big mom
Support and comfort bring.

I never did realize
Until this very day
That that feeling of power
Has lead me astray.

It has produced in me
"Delusions of grandeur,"
Thinking myself great
And all others insecure.

Bring me back to earth.
Lord, help me to see
It's You and Your power that's great.

Lead me to embrace others,
Not considering myself superior,
And from them not isolate.

$\mathscr{O}$ SOLATION

Found myself in a space
Where I did not
Feel part of the human race.

Where connection
Was lacking,
And so was any real direction.

I did not bond well from the start
With the people I called my folks.
Satan with evil thoughts,
He eventually tried to coax.

Seeds, thoughts of suicide
He planted within.
He'd say that if I do it,
I could be free.

Free from worldly torment
And the things that got me down.
That it would promise to relieve
Me of my perpetual frown.

Such seeds caused me, though,
To further isolate.
A downward spiral
They did precipitate.

Deeper I would go
Into my own little world.
The seeds, they'd grow and grow
Till I got overwhelmed

And attacked to such an extent
That he made suicide seem
Like the only option,
The very best thing to do.

The devil, he's tricky and powerful,
A formidable foe.
Jesus had to die so agonizingly
To right Satan's wrong, don't you know?

Isolation he uses
To pull me from that which
Can strengthen, give hope.

The devil will pull me
From Jesus to himself
And take me to the end of my rope.

Then the temptations pour in.
Be very careful
Of this one called Satan,

For he will urge you to do
Things you normally wouldn't do.
Beware of isolation, his tool
To get you to harm yourself and others too.

The Pull of Home

Happy or sad.
Good or bad.
There is a pull of home, for true

Home life beckons,
And it reckons
To be recreated by you.

If turmoil you did have,
Then unconsciously for real
You may go around
Reliving the same deal.

For it's very hard to know,
To gain insight, to grow.
Not to let the unconscious rule,
God led me to relationship school.

For me, it was counseling*
That helped me understand
How, for instance, I saw
My father in every single man.

I find, since turmoil was the norm,
That I am at home in a storm.
I did cling

To those that sting,
As unhealthy relationships I did form.

For home has a pull
That's deeper than deep.
It'll run your life.
It'll play for keeps.

So, Lord, help me
To reach out and be
Brave to take the steps,
As beyond home I need to get.

---

*Prov. 11:14, 24:6, 12:15.

HURT FEELINGS

Wear them 'round your neck
For everyone to see.
Wear them on your arm,
With your heart on your sleeve.

Or keep your feelings in tight,
Never digging deep to say
That pain that you keep hidden,
Find it hard to articulate.

"Come to me, but go away.
In my heart you cannot stay.
Have no room for you,
For my hurts I cherish, I do.

I cling to my hurts;
They serve me well.
The definition of strong
Is not to talk or to tell."

But I say to you that
Into the hands of God
Is where those hurts really belong.

To bring them forward
And to face them
Is what truly makes you strong.

That would give God
A chance to make it right.
You could give Him your hurts
Instead of holding them tight.

Maybe you hold them in
Because you are afraid
That He might require of you
A working through to be made.

"I just though seem to sit
On a fence between hot and cold.
Can't take that step of faith.
Days pass, and I grow old.

Lukewarm* I guess I am.
I guess I do need to grow.
Beyond this wall I've erected,
I see now I need to go."

---

* "So, because you are lukewarm—neither hot nor cold—I
am about to spit you out of my mouth" (Rev. 3:16).

PART II

ON RELATING TO OTHERS

PARALYSIS OF THE WILL

I have a friend
Who's stuck in a rut,
Deeply burrowed down.

He can't find his way.
He's wrapped in chains,
Feels trapped within a frown.

For he carries with him
Bag upon bag of care.
In his unconscious,
It's deeply hidden there,

Just out of reach,
Just out of view.
God, take him
On a way that's new.

'Cause the weight of that baggage,
It paralyzes his will.
We try to help,
But he persists still.

In carrying his luggage,
Not unloading and unpacking it,
He's working so hard,
He just won't quit.

Oh, help him surrender
It all, Lord, to You,
So You can shoulder
And carry it too.

Then You can lead him
To help, to good counsel
All those years of holding it in,
That guilt You can surely cancel.

He's too strong to be weak.
Do cause him to see
You and I and help he needs
To live interdependently.

SEPARATE

I am separate
From the one I love.
I feel so unbearably sad.

You help me tolerate
My searing aloneness.
You come in and live inside.

And You say that
You will never leave
Nor forsake me ever.

Thank You that You stay
Right next to my broken heart.
Oh, it needs You so.

For in my pain, I am prone
To wander, to stray.
Help me cling to You, Jesus, my comfort,
With all my might today.

⊘DE TO ⏉ACK

Burdened with a family
Who don't know how to care
About the things that move Jack's heart.
They really don't dare …

… dare to enter in.
They stay on the sidelines.
He's a psych patient—
That is his crime.

They live in caves, hiding.
Live in busyness, striving.
Not offering a hand to hold.
Inside they are distant, cold.

For he is a mental patient
To them and always will be
Debilitated, struck down,
Vulnerable, and weak.

Look down on him they do;
As an equal he's not seen.
In a psych ward and a mental hospital,
That's where he's been.

So he's judged for
This biochemical illness of his

Not of his own making,
But of God's it ultimately is.

Yet on solid ground,
Jack stands on the Rock.*
He seeks help from his Creator
And from his trusted doc.

He works things through
When he gets tired or overwhelmed.
He knows where to go
For help in the psychiatric realm.

He's braver than he knows.
He takes his illness and grows.
He talks about his feelings too.
All the right things he does do.

Jack may be your neighbor.
He's not so far from you.
So look upon this man named Jack—
You might just learn a thing or two.

Think twice when you
Cross him on the street.
He is truly among the most
Honorable men you could meet.

---

* "Trust in the Lord forever, for the Lord, the Lord himself, is the Rock eternal" (Isa. 26:4).

A Connection

They work in the institution,
And every day they find
Overwhelming needs.

Each day they come,
Many can do little more
Than the basic physical deeds.

Many come in and out,
Just doing the physical task.
They cannot engage with me;
I have to wear a mask.

A mask that says all is great.
The nurses, they reign.
When all is said and done,
It's they who have their way.

Oh, we can complain,
But it's virtually useless,
For the complaints procedure
Is a circular process.

Because the needs in this place
Are so overwhelmingly huge,
The workers find it hard to smile
And face the day as new.

For they deal with the needy.
Some nurses spurn them, they do.
Spurn them for their vulnerability
That touches a part in them too.

That part in them
That makes them feel small.
That part in them
That they find hard to tolerate at all.

Oh, you caregivers,
I really do thank you
For what you do for this vulnerable one.

But won't you
Step out and try
To make a human connection?

An Abandoning Person

"Weak one,
I find you too much.
I cannot reach out,
Your heart to touch.

For you trigger something deep inside
That I just cannot stand.
The little person in me
That makes me feel less of a woman, less of a man.

I want to engage,
But deep down within,
I can't get it right.
I really can't win.

Have no room to care
For your troubles and woes,
Wrapped up in my own.
That's how it goes.

So go I must,
And go I will.
I know you need me.
I have to go still."

*O*DE TO THE *N*URSES

Such difficult work
Is what you do,
Cleaning up messes
We leave for you.

You persevere,
Even despite
Difficult patients
That test your might.

Some of them do
Test you, it's true,
For they have so many needs.

But thanks I do say
And applaud you today.
For I couldn't do without you, indeed.

Six Arms and as Many Legs: Ode to the Nurses

Six arms and as many legs
Is what I feel I need
To accomplish the task
That God sets before me.

I have a good day
When most things go okay,
But there are days when
So much goes wrong, and then

Then I want to scream
Or maybe have a good cry.
Stocks are low or out,
And the in-charge makes me sigh.

At home too, I have
Troubles that are real.
Hard not to bring
Them to work, I feel.

In many directions
I'm being pulled
Sometimes, for true.

God, help me
Keep it together
To serve my patients, to serve You.*

---

* "Truly I tell you, whatever you did for one of the least of these brothers and sisters of mine, you did for me" (Matt. 25:40).

OPPRESSION

One thing the vulnerable
In particular can find.
Some can take chunks out of them.

From the ones to whom they are close
To nurses and attendants that "help"
To the driver of the specialized bus.

The vulnerable can be a conduit,
A dumping zone,
A punching bag.

When this happens
To me personally,
I can feel like a useless rag.

For each of the vulnerable is a person
Made of flesh and blood
With feelings and wishes and dreams.

The way we occasionally
Find ourselves treated
Can really be quite mean.

Because we are different,
You feel heavy when us you see.
But hey, don't disrespectful
Or hasty or impatient be.

'Cause when you and we cross paths,
Jesus said, and you'll see,
"Whatever you did for the least of these …
You did for me."*

---

* Matt. 25:40; "Whoever oppresses the poor shows contempt for their Maker, but whoever is kind to the needy honors God" (Prov. 14:31).

OVERGIVING

You give and you give and you give,
More than what's healthy.
Fear of anger and of abandonment—
That's where you live.

"If I give, they won't get mad."
"If I give, they won't leave me."
"If I give, they'll need me."
Those are your heart's pleas.

"Please love me."
"Please need me."
"Please think I'm good."

These and more
Are what's going on
Beneath the hood.

You need to learn to take in and receive
Good things for yourself in this life.
You so deserve good things.
You deserve much more than just strife.

Now, it's fine to give—in fact it's better.*
Where would the world be if we did not?

But don't give out of fear, but out of love.
"God is Love,"** and it's free! He cannot be bought.

---

* "It is more blessed to give than to receive" (Acts 20:35).
**1 John 4:8b, 16b.

DENIAL

Denial is a demon
That takes you away.
It keeps you in a box,
Out of touch, in the gray.

It seems to protect you,
I really must say,
From the nasty truth
You find so hard to face.

But truth is truth regardless;
Endlessly it marches on,
Day after day after day.

It knocks now and then
To try to gain entry in
To your troubled heart.

If you would but listen
And let it in more,
Then we could make a start.

But in denial you remain,
And I who yearn to help
Stay "unemployed" and sad.

You won't let me in;
Independence your god.
It's all you've ever known or had.

What you need
Is interdependence
And to break the barriers down.

So can we work together
On this problem so big?
I know a solution can eventually be found.

Just Like You

Don'tcha know
I'm just like you?

You call me disabled;
I look different too.

But don'tcha know
I'm just like you?

I live in a chair
From a spinal cord injury.
It could happen to you; that aside,
You're really no different than me.

I suffer like you do.
I rejoice like you too.
I dare to dream as well

About a spouse,
About a house,
About excitement to tell.

Some days I wish there were
More in my life who reach out
Beyond the metal frame

To see that I have
Strengths to offer,
Though I may be lame.

I hurt just like you.
When you pass me by,
Do you shake your head
Or, in pity, whisper, "My, my"?

Get to know the disabled.
They're profound and deep.
They make the best friend.
They are faithful for keeps.

They have their cross.
You have one too.

Don'tcha know?
We're just like you.

CONTAGIOUS

Contagious.
It's outrageous
But oh, so true.

Evil and goodness—
All of it, no less—
Has a ripple effect from me to you.

For good promotes good.
When you witness true love,
You'll want to know
What those folk are made of.

With evil,
It's the same.
With evil,
It's no game.

A complaining spirit
Is like a cold, damp cloth
That spreads all around.

Gossip can lead to more,
And before you know it,
Someone is literally torn down.

With suicide, there's a ripple effect
If a crack in the foundation you do detect,
It can lead to all crumbling down,
Result in rubble right to the ground.

Remember that suicide does leave
A trail of folks who grieve,
And it really could inspire
Another to suicide, to conspire.

I know you may be
In unrelenting pain.
Know we are blessed, though,
By your movement forward again.

How you get there is to know
That it's especially at the onset
Of bad news that the pain is most intense.

If you endure
Even minute by minute,
You'll find in time things'll make more sense.

So what I am saying is this:
Remember that in all you do,
People are watching and waiting.
They might follow your example, good or bad, too.

WAITING

Tick, tock.
Tick, tock.
The minutes, the hours, the days go by,
And I get ever older and closer to the grave.

In silence I wait,
Wait for word from you, of you.
Lord, You say not to have anyone above You.
And with my dear one, I get tempted …

… tempted to worry, that weed called worry.
… tempted to fear, which is not of You.
… tempted to listen to the whispers of the enemy, who
Tells me all is awry.

(Even if things did not go my way,
And word from You, of You was bad,
It would still stand true
That not all has gone awry.)

And yet I wait.
I try to be patient; a hero I'm not.
I bite my nails, and yet
I try to think happy thoughts.*

You, Father, are the Great Waiter.
You waited thirty-three long years
To be with Your Son again physically.

You waited and watched Him grow
From a helpless baby with human parents
To the Man who would teach us how to love.

You waited while He was brutalized,
Ripped and torn at, His flesh crucified.
Yet You did not intervene until it was finished.

Spiritually, You and He were one all along!
Grow me up to be more like You and Your dear Son,
That I might have Your strength, Father, to continue to
wait.

---

* "Finally, brothers and sisters, whatever is true, whatever
is noble, whatever is right, whatever is pure, whatever is
lovely, whatever is admirable—if anything is excellent or
praiseworthy—think about such things" (Phil. 4:8).

A FRIEND

Met with a friend, I did.
But all he did was hid.
Hid from facing the truth,
Really acted like a kid.

He's fully grown,
All of forty-three.
Don't know what You hold
Down the road for him and me.

A Christian he is, and yet he chooses
Not Your way but his own.
Still, even after a bad fall,
Aimlessly he does roam.

He no longer reaches out
To me nor really to You.
He's stuck in self-loathing
Despite what You're trying to do.

I feel sad that
My friend cannot see
And experience Your love.

Lord, lasso him.
Bring him back
To seeking and looking to You from above.

ON DAD

You rocked my world with violence.
You left me high and dry.
You walked out of my life.
I locked up deep inside.

I became numb to you
And my mother too.
They never learned Your love,
So I did not feel it from You.

Unapproachable they both were.
My childhood a blur
Of rage, of hate, of untamed emotions.
My music became my sole devotion.

As a teen, I wanted to know you, Dad,
Instead of walking around all sad.
So pursue you I did,
But from me you hid.

We got together, yes,
And I was thankful for this.
You couldn't give what you never had:
The love that was alone His.

Then in my twenties, I found God;
Jesus revealed to me His love.

He taught that He was it,
That all good things came from above.

Many decades later,
At seventy-nine years of age,
You asked me
About this God I knew.

Right then and there,
You embraced Jesus,
The very love of *my* heart.

You accepted Him,
And from that
You made a new start.

"You're teaching me
How to love," years later
You, Dad, said to me.

For that,
For all you've become,
You are now so dear and always will be.

PART III

ON HOPE IN JESUS

LEANING ON JESUS

This is a scary, wonderful thing
To lean wholly on my Savior.
There are so many other things
That try to draw me in.

Money tempts me to cling to it.
So do the structures around me.
I know that You alone keep my world
From crumbling into dust.

Tsunamis, earthquakes, hurricanes—
You have at your beck and call.
One word from You,
And You could take it all.

My health too lies precariously
In Your hands, for true.
I cannot make it an idol,
For You could take it too.

So trust You I will.
I'll cleave to You still.
For that is the only way

To preserve my peace.
For You never cease
To give me Your strength just for today.*

---

* "[D]o not worry about tomorrow, for tomorrow will worry about itself. Each day has enough trouble of its own" (Matt. 6:34).

FOOD: A TEMPTING PANACEA

Dear Lord:

You know how I struggle
When things go wrong.
Can give in to food.
Can't seem to stay strong.

God's diet plan
Is discipline, so
Charles Stanley has said.

But in stress, I can reach
For sweets, for goodies,
Foregoing discipline instead.

I need Your strength to resist
Satan's tempting spread,
That which is so readily available

In this culture I have,
Though others have not.
Please make me capable

Of thinking more globally
And not just of myself.
With Your help, those cookies
Will stay on the shelf. Amen.

FLOWERS IN THE DESERT

I have a little cactus,
All prickly and tough.
Bristles and leather skin—
That's what it's made of.

On its surface
Grow star-shaped thorns.
All symmetrical, each one
Growing from a single skin horn.

But its exterior betrays it,
For from deep down within
Spring nine pink blossoms
From deep beneath the prickly skin.

Nine radiant blossoms
In all pink, yellow, and white.
It really is
Quite a delightful sight.*

I am like a cactus,
All prickly and tough.
But from deep down within
Is growing beauty and such,

Such like I've never seen
Or could never believe to be.

Out of my barren desert,
A lush garden grows in me.

So if you're dry,
Just know
That spiritual
Flowers can grow

Where and when
You least expect,
The creator of whom
May be God, I suspect.§

---

*An actual plant.

§ This was written when I was new to the wheelchair and living in the institution. Subsequently, I had developed some doubt about the very existence of a loving God.

HARDER TO HOLD

It's getting increasingly
Harder to hold
On to Your hand.

Cruelty of thought and deed
From ones who claim to be
My very siblings in Christ.

Abandonment of Scripture,
Their hearts backslidden,
They seem to fail to see

And cannot abide by the conviction
Of the very Holy Spirit
That breathes life and love into me.

They turn from the face of God.
I cannot just stand by.
God, redeem them, enlighten them
To the error of their ways.

You have taught us to
"Love your enemies, and pray
For those who persecute You."†
Only with Your help can I do this today.

Their behavior drives me,
I find, to seek answers
To the questions I thought
You and I had already resolved.

It's getting increasingly
Harder to hold
On to Your hand.

Their betrayal
Tempts me also,
Not by my Lord to stand.

Oh, still I can choose
Your help, Lord, to ask:
Keep my hand in Yours
And strengthen my grasp.

---

† Matt. 5:44.

OUR POWER SOURCE

Just like the TV
Needs to be
Plugged in to work;

Just like the nerves
In limbs need to be
Connected to the
Spinal cord to function;

Just like the branch
Needs to be
Attached to the vine
To receive nutrients and live;

So we need to be
Connected to Jesus
For the Holy Spirit
To abide in us.

God is our power source.
We need to remain in Jesus*
For Him to be able
To produce fruit in us.

Do get and stay connected
To our Creator.†

Surrender and let the Spirit
Take full control.

---

* "I am the vine; you are the branches. If you remain in me and I in you, you will bear much fruit; apart from me you can do nothing" (John 15:5).

† "For in him all things were created: things in heaven and on earth, visible and invisible, whether thrones or powers or rulers or authorities; all things were created through him and for him. He is before all things, and in him all things hold together" (Col. 1:16–17).

ON THANKFULNESS

Don'tcha know
It's good to grow
In thankfulness?

Be thankful
In all things*
So hard to express.

In blue skies,
In butterflies,
In wonderful highs,
In baby's cries.

In dark days,
In purple haze,
In a painful phase,
In bright and warm Mays.**

In the good and the painful,
Don't turn away, be disdainful.
But give thanks to God.
You He will applaud.

---

*1 Thess. 5:18.

**Written in an unseasonably cold and dreary April.

HIS-TUNES

What frequency are you on?
What do you listen to?
Do you tune into the Spirit?
Is there God's flow in you?

Do you hum a God song
As you go your merry way?
Do you listen to Him,
What He wants and tries to say?

Or do you let the noise
Of the world distract and diffuse?
Maybe even noise as a
Buffer from God you use?

For God can tell us
And show us things
That cause us great pain.

To stay with Him
And ride it out
Can bring us, though, ultimately great gain.

But it can be tempting
To veer away,
To get caught up
In the world's way.

As Danny Brooks sings,
"Lord, fence me in."
I want to stay in the flow
And hear Your Holy Spirit tunes within.

A Spiritual Suicide

When I say
"Don't give up,"
What does come to mind?

You think perhaps
Of the ultimate
"Giving up"—you think of suicide.

But let me say
That there are ways
Of giving up for true

That do not involve
A made resolve
To end the life that's you.

For you can give up and remain
In the very flesh you call home.
You can abandon Christ
And let yourself freely roam.

Roam into waywardness,
Roam into sin.
Won't come near Jesus.
Won't let Him deeply in.

"For I want a way
That is my very own.
Don't want Jesus
To make in me His home.

I want what I want.
Nothing else will do.
You can let Jesus lead;
That's okay for you."

Give up on God
While living in your skin?
Choosing your own sweet way?

This is a death,
A spiritual suicide.
Won't you turn back to Him now, today?

Clinging to Him
In this world of care
Is in this life the only sure way.

Do it for yourself.
Face Him once again.
For He longs to commune with you
And be your closest, everlasting Friend.

Sharpness: The Result of Courage

Lately I've been
So burdened with care
That I retreated

Into sleep,
Into laziness.
Kind of felt defeated.

Wanted to ignore
All the trouble for sure.
Felt like facing it
Wasn't the cure.

But when finally
I did get up and go,
I realized I was dulled
By that laziness, you know.

For there is a sharpness
That comes when we face
Our pain, our trials head-on.

To make the decision,
To retreat—in hindsight
I may have been wrong.

We all get tired
And are tempted to give in.
Help us, though,
Not to involve sin.

Slothfulness doesn't fit us
As children of God.
I do know our courage
You, Jesus, quietly applaud.

SPIRITUAL OBESITY

Spiritual obesity—
I see it everywhere.
People living in a way that
They really don't care.

Don't care for their neighbors.
Don't care for themselves.
They leave good nutrition
And exercise on the shelf.

Hoarding the carnal
And that which they lust.
No room for God,
No room for trust.

Wasting time on the frivolous.
Talking, not saying much.
Allowing self-pity,
Blaming, and such.

I feel sad
When I see someone
In this state.

Open their eyes,
Show Yourself
To be the one who's great.

Great at love
And wisdom too.
All they need is
To give their heart to You.

For You transform
The self-loathing,
The shame, the pain

Into peace
And freedom
And hope once again.

So free up souls
Who are caught in a mire.
Set hearts ablaze,
Set them on fire.

TIME

Time proceeds
Relentlessly.

It forges on
Through a storm,
Through the rain,
With the sun.

It doesn't stop
For hurricanes,
For earthquakes,
For natural and
Personal disasters.

It doesn't stop
When the integrity
Of our bodies fail.

It plows right along
Through weddings,
Through funerals.
It is no respecter of events.

Seems like the more we enjoy,
The faster it goes.
And when we want it to speed up,
It crawls at a snail's pace.

Time can be
Glorious friend
Or hated foe.

Especially in the afterlife,
Depends on
To which place we will go.

Though time is relentless,
It'll all but come to an end.
Time as we know it
We will all but spend.

Eternal—I can't fathom.
But that's the deal.
Our souls, ourselves
Will spend it somewhere.

And on a decision*
It will all hinge
Whether we will go on
In torment or in bliss.

Turn and trust.
I've said it before.
To be assured a place in heaven,
Surrender your heart to His.

*"If you declare with your mouth, 'Jesus is Lord,' and believe in your heart that God raised him from the dead, you will be saved" (Rom.10:9); "Jesus replied, 'Very truly I tell you, no one can see the kingdom of God unless they are born again'" (John 3:3).

I wrote the following trilogy post-injury when Jesus delivered me on a new level from a heavy burden I had carried.

$\mathcal{S}$WEET $\mathcal{F}$REEING $\mathcal{J}$ESUS

Sweet freeing Jesus,
You make my heart sing.
Close to Your breast
Forever will I cling.

I am so glad
To be able to say
That I love You more dearly
Than ever today.

For You free me from chains
And fetters so strong.
You knew it was wrong
For me to live with them on.

You helped me shout, "Freedom!"
And throw them aside.
Near by Your side
You ask me to abide.

For relentless is evil,
So relentless I'll be—

At seeking You first,*
Learning more what it is to be free.

So thank You, dear Savior,
For helping me to see
That I was meant for You,
And You were meant for me.

---

* "But seek first his kingdom and his righteousness, and
all these things will be given to you as well" (Matt. 6:33).

FLYING WITH JESUS

Flying I do,
I float like a bird,
Soaring high above,
Singing songs yet unheard.

Flying, I feel free
And truly happy.
Didn't know, wouldn't believe
That such freedom I could receive.

You heal me, You do.
I know that it's true,
And I'll never be the same.

Thank You for mending.
Thank You, Father, for sending
Jesus—truly the Name above any other name.

JESUS FREES US

Jesus frees us,
Sends us soaring
To heights and special places.

He kindles and rekindles
The fire within and
Brings us into wide open spaces,

Where He can show us
The truth of who we are
As individuals, as Christians.
He brings near what was far,

Far out of reach,
Or so I thought.
To search in and up
Is what He's taught.

I really cannot say
Nor adequately put into words
All that I feel,
All that I've heard …

… heard from Jesus
As He teaches me His way.
With Him forever
I know I will stay.

CROUTINE

I live in a world of routine
Where regimentation rules,
But that, in fact, can be seen
As the very tool

That God uses to produce
Endurance of spirit and faith,
Endurance of heart.
A toughness it makes,

Resiliency of spirit.
Not hardness, though.
He makes you a conduit
As you let His love flow.

You need to know
And be able to discern
What to take in, when to say no.
You really need to learn

To let in and let out
Just like a breath.
Take in the good
And discard the rest.*

Routine is there, yes,
But we need a balance to strike

Between work and play,
Between fun and strife.

A balanced routine—
That's how we become
A diamond; it's coal under pressure.

A flower will wilt
And eventually give way
To fruit, then seed that is hidden treasure.

For from a single seed,
Many more can come.
So let go and let God work
Right till He's done.

For it is through
Structure and healthy routine
That perseverance, character,
And hope** can be seen.

---

* When the devil puts thoughts in your mind—something
you cannot stop him from doing—let them come and go.
Do not dwell or linger on the negative thought.

** [W]e … glory in our sufferings, because we know
that suffering produces perseverance; perseverance,
character; and character, hope" (Rom. 5:3–4).

FACING MYSELF

Facing myself—
It's the hardest thing
To hear the music
And let it sing.

Not just hearing
But listening too, you see.
To all that's going on
Deep inside of me.

I find I cannot know
What is beneath the surface
Until I let someone in
To help me handle the mess.

The mess that is pain,
The mess that is rage.
I needed godly counsel
In order to turn the page,

To go from pain to peace,
To find some resolution.
Seeking a Christian counselor
Has been a real solution.

For facing myself
And the hurt deep within

Is so difficult, takes God
To keep me from sin.

Lord, I don't want the rage
To come out in other ways.
As it comes up, help me face it
And not run away and quit.

Let me be brave, then,
To endure the process and step out.
I can find freedom with help—
That I truly won't doubt.

LOVE AFFAIR

You say you are not in love,
But I beg to differ.
You are in a love affair
Of one sort or another.

Is it independence? Is it fear?
Is it the bottle or the drugs?
Is it tobacco or is it caffeine?
Or is it another in codependence?

Love is what we're about as humans.
It's what we share; it's what we crave.
But I caution you
Not to cling to anything

Or anyone more than
You do to Jesus.
Choose Jesus to adore.
Make Him first, I implore.

And let Him carry
Your trials,
Even yourself,
As in "Footprints."*

A faithful God
He really is,

But you must choose with whom and with what
You have your greatest love affair.

Love† and receive Him,
The Creator of your soul,
And He will in turn give to you
Riches‡ untold.

---

* "Footprints" by Margaret Fishback Powers.

† "You shall have no other gods before me" (Deut. 5:7); "'Love the Lord your God with all your heart and with all your soul and with all your mind.' This is the first and greatest commandment" (Matt. 22:37–38).

‡ God may not choose to give riches of the material kind, but spiritually He can bestow them on any believer following closely after Him, as in salvation and the fruits of the Spirit: "love, joy, peace, forbearance, kindness, goodness, faithfulness, gentleness and self-control" (Gal. 5:22–23a).

CHOOSING REAL LIFE

"We pause for a moment
To honor the fallen
On this Remembrance Day.*

We interrupt this program
To bring you a few images
Of war and of its way.

Way of destruction,
Of horror, of terror.
Do bear with and stay …

… stay on this channel
Just for a moment.
Then we return you
To your regular show,

To that which makes
You feel better,
Feel more comfortable.
You are free to go."

For me, I choose
Real life.
I choose to recall
The horror, the strife

Not only of war
But of all the deep pain
On this dark earth.
Dark stories and again

Of abuse, of rape,
Of incest, of greed,
And all of the sins from which
We can ultimately be freed.

I don't live in the darkness,
But touch it I will.
My Savior heals and comforts.
My heart is genuinely filled.

For it was for real life,
To defeat "the prince of this world,"**
That Jesus died and rose again.
To eternal darkness, the devil was hurled.

Praise Jesus,
The one, the only.
His life, His light

Makes it possible to face real life,
Including the devil, his demons,
And all their diabolical might.

———————————————

* Written 11/11/11.

** John 14:30.

A Gentleman

Jesus is a gentleman.
He doesn't take over and step in.
He asks us merely to come
Come and follow Him.

He gently leads
So quietly and softly too.
He does it so tenderly
Look! He even calls you!

He will not force
Himself on anyone,
But He doesn't stop calling
Till your life is done.

For suffering and dying
Are yet but tools
He uses to draw you near,

To break down anger,
To fill you with wonder,
To help you face your deepest fear.

Deep suffering
A precious gift;
With it He truly
Wants to lift,

Lift you up
To even higher ground.
With Him is where you belong.

That's why it urges
In Scripture time and again.
Be courageous and be strong.*

For Jesus is a gentleman.
He only whispers to you.
He asks you to listen
And then obey Him too.

You can choose
To go your own sweet way,
But you reap what you sow†
Both now and on Judgment Day.‡

---

*Deut. 31:6-7, 23; Josh. 1:7, 9, 18; Josh. 10:25; 1 Chron. 22:13; 1 Chron. 28:20; 2 Chron. 32:7.

† "Do not be deceived: God cannot be mocked. A man reaps what he sows" (Gal. 6:7); "Remember this: whoever sows sparingly will also reap sparingly, and whoever sows generously will also reap generously" (2 Cor. 9:6).

‡ "For God will bring every deed into judgment, including every hidden thing, whether it is good or evil" (Eccles. 12:14); "[P]eople are destined to die once, and after that to face judgment" (Heb. 9:27).

Heaven on Earth

My soul craves heaven.
From this earthly prison
I sometimes want a way out.

Now coming to Alaska,
I've seen heaven on earth;
I can proclaim it with a shout.

Between mountains high,
This ship does make its way
Through the passage along its route.

I found a spot to myself
Where I can lay
My burdens on the shelf

And spread out my hands
With palms facing up.
With you, dear Jesus,
Will I dance and sup.

Enjoying spiritual and real food
Of the smorgasbord type,
I take in my fill
And ignore all the hype.

The drinking, the gambling,
The immorality, the illicit sex—
So much of it too on this cruise.

And yet He gives to me
His grandeur, His majesty.
Of this, I richly and fully peruse.

Because I've seen
A bit of heaven on earth,
And through all this, dear Jesus,
You show me my great worth.

My great worth
You reveal to me.
I know now I feel
Even more free.

Free to commit
More deeply than ever
To life, to this journey,
For now and into forever.

SAFE IN JESUS

I notice within myself
That the familiar can become
A cave in which I live,
A cave to which I succumb.

I retreat to this cave,
For me, it's the result of abuse.
Spent years in this space;
It gives me a short fuse.

I retreat to this cave
Despite a call to change.
For this feels "safe," home to me.

Fear stands between
Me and the unknown.
Brave now I really must be.

Lo and behold,
I look, and You extending
Your Hand is what I see,

Gently urging me forward
Through my fear
To take that step of faith

Into the light
Your true light,
Where I am truly and genuinely safe.

GRACE

As I follow me through my day,
I sense myself going under
A mass of various emotions
I cannot keep track of.

But grace holds me firm.
Yes, the anchor does hold.
The miracle of salvation.
The miracle of the Holy Spirit in me.

Grace encompasses,
Keeps me buoyant
When all around
Feels a crashing mess.

I am so blessed
To have Jesus as my Savior,
The one who works
In me on my behalf.*

Please never leave!
With You inside me,
I find I can truly laugh
Even when all goes wrong.

For You and Your grace
Bring hope when I truly let

You be You, for You are
My joy incarnate.

Help me, dear Jesus,
To let Your grace reign.
Cause me to be patient, gentle, loving
Again and again and again.

---

* "Since ancient times no one has heard, no ear has perceived, no eye has seen any God besides you, who acts on behalf of those who wait for him" (Isa. 64:4).

SUBSTITUTE SAVIORS

"You've got to go to the lonesome valley;
No one can go there for you.

You've got to go to the lonesome valley;
No one can go there for you."*

What do you lean on?
Would it be sex?
Would it be a john?

Booze, other people, your own will?
Do you rely at your core
On these things still?

What do you clutch?
What is your crutch
To help you get by?
Do you live in a lie?

Hatred, bitterness, rage—
These can take us away.
Hanging on to these,
Crippled we will stay.

Substitute saviors
Don't properly fill the hole.
It's only through Jesus

That we become spiritually whole.

Our best is not enough;
We need forgiveness for sin.
He alone can heal the state,
The condition we find ourselves in.

For "you've got to go to the lonesome valley;
No one can go there for you.

You've got to go to the lonesome valley;
No one can go there for you."

---

* "Lonesome Valley" by Fairfield Four, from the *O Brother, Where Art Thou?* soundtrack.

ℬREATH

I have breath.
I have been given breath.
I can breathe
And feel free

To be what I am.
Lost at times,
Sinner always,
I am free to be me.

Just me,
Simple and true.
I'm not anyone else.
I'm not you.

But you as well can be
Free and hopeful too.
You can find peace
In what you are and do.

I pray His peace
Upon your ways.
If with Him you abide,
With you He stays.*

Look in and up,
And you will find

Hope everlasting
In body, soul, and mind.

Trust me today,
'Cause I think I've found the way
To make life so worthwhile.

I really do believe
If Him you receive,
He will turn your frown to a smile.†

---

* "Remain in me, as I also remain in you" (John 15:4a).

† "He [the Lord] has sent me [literally referring to a prophet] ... to bestow on them ... the oil of joy instead of mourning" (Isa. 61:1b, 3b, 3c).

MY ONLY HOPE

I recall my long stay
In the institution, on the ward.
You were my only hope.
You and You alone, Lord.

For I had to hear
The words of those near.
Secondhand conversations
Caused me such frustrations.

The people in the hall
Made such a racket for true.
So hard to find some
Quiet space for me and for You.

A quiet little space
Is all I wanted to find.
On God's green earth,
Away from the daily grind

Of the institution;
No one could flourish there.
I felt like I needed
Maybe whiskey, maybe beer.

What I had and have is Someone,
Jesus Christ, my Savior.

To Him I'll cling
And pray all the more.

Because He is strength
And He is hope.
With Him alone
Is how I'd cope.

Sometimes it seems
That He doesn't do that much.
He doesn't take away
The pain or the suffering as such.*

But with it He molds.
He strengthens, He does.
So go on, dear Jesus. Just help me

To seek You
All the time,
For my only hope rests in Thee.

---

*About a year or so after I wrote this poem, I was interviewed and accepted to an organization that trained disabled people to live independently in apartment settings. God proved His faithfulness despite my difficulty at the time in seeing beyond my circumstances.

I FOLDED MY HANDS

I folded my hands to pray.
I was in a prison.
I reached to the Son,
Who died and had Risen.

I asked him
His strength to give
To endure the bars,
To help me live.

The prison bars faded
In the light of Him
As the world around me
Grew remarkably dim.

All I could see
While being in the light
Was Him and Him alone.
It almost filled me with fright.

For He is so real
Or has made Himself to be.
Jesus is my hope.
Stay, dear Lord, always near me.

A Christmas Poem

Come one, come all,
And celebrate the birth
Of our dear Savior
With merriment and mirth.

You know it truly is
A time to give God thanks
For all that He has done.

It was, after all, through Him
That was granted to us
Our oh so precious salvation.

But if you find yourself
Not merry but more blue,
Know it's okay
To feel as you do.

Friends can forsake.
Family can too.
Perhaps it's an anniversary
Of a sad occasion for you.

Maybe just getting together
Certain relatives you rarely see
May tend to produce within you
More than a bit of misery.

Give it to Jesus,
Whatever you feel,
And He will make
His dear Presence real.

Comfort He will bestow
On all who draw near.
He can soothe a heavy heart.
He can wipe away each tear.

Whatever your emotional state,
Try to rejoice at Him coming as a baby.
He died and rose to give us joy that can be our strength,*
That can make us soar through it all: Yes! Not maybe.

---

* "The thief comes only to steal and kill and destroy; I
have come that they may have life, and have it to the full"
(John 10:10); "[T]he joy of the Lord is ... (our) strength"
(Neh. 8:10).

Approaching Spring

The thaw is on, in more ways than one,
On our streets and in our hearts.
Trickle of activity as folks start
To shake off the winter blahs.

Heavy coats are shed;
Hats and mittens too.
There is an aliveness in the air
For me and for you.

Birds are singing and seem
To be flying more free
As the great weight of winter
Comes off them and me.

For the world is awakening
From a slumber, a cold.
It's putting on the new
And shedding the old.

Trees are coming to bud,
And the sun again feels warm,
Replacing with a lightness
The deep, dark snow storm

That was so ominous
Just a few short weeks ago.

Now there are everywhere
Rivers of melting snow.

I never did appreciate,
Or feel quite so strong,
The newness of the day
As it gets progressively long.

For You mold something
Through the winter of our souls
That brings life and love anew.

Please help me, Jesus,
Understand Your ways,
Or at least in all see You.

UNACCESSIBILITY

Buildings I see,
Stairs and more stairs
Adding to my cares.

For me, as one
Who lives her life
In a chair,

I watch as
People can look down
In more ways than one.

Jesus can help us overcome*
The barriers in our hearts.
He's freely loving
Right from the start.

And He helps us to be
In His love and feel free.
Free to reach and take a stand
For justice, for every woman, child, and man.

So when you approach me in my chair,
Open your heart, please do.
Aside from an injury to my spine,
I'm really just like you.

---

* "In this world you will have trouble. But take heart! I have overcome the world" (John 16:33).

HIS ETERNAL NATURE

His eternal nature is not
Totally accessible to the finite mind.
For His ways, His thoughts
Are unique, are one of a kind.†

But ask your questions,
Your why ones too.
In Him are still the answers
For both me and for you.

And when you don't find answers
To all God says and does,
Know that faith is the bridge,
And in mystery still lies love.

---

† "For my thoughts are not your thoughts, neither are your ways my ways,' declares the Lord" (Isa. 55:8).

Secret Sin

Secret sin—
Is there such a thing?

What do you find yourself doing?
Know that Jesus is still wooing
You back to Himself
He wants that sin to go back on the shelf.

What is needed is that
You get clean through and through,
And that is something
That only Jesus can do.

You need to go to Him
In repentance and holy fear.*
He's the one to heal.
He'll wipe every tear.†

For He knows you
Completely, He alone
To Him your sin
Is thoroughly known.

It's your relationship
To Him that matters truly.
You need to get right with Him;
Then you can come to me.

Confess your sins,
One to another.‡
Seek God first,
Then go to your brother.

Whatever it is,
It grieves Him so.
Won't you into
His hands, I urge you, let it go?

---

* "The fear of the Lord is the beginning of wisdom" (Ps. 111:10a).

† "The Sovereign Lord will wipe away the tears from all faces" (Isa. 25:8); "And God will wipe away every tear from their eyes" (Rev. 7:17c).

‡ "Therefore confess your sins to each other and pray for each other so that you may be healed" (James 5:16).

CONFINEMENT

Confined
In my body
And in my mind.

For I want to fly,
But for real, can I
With a heart so prone to fear?

It can hold me back
And keep me in the black
As I shed, it seems, tear upon tear.

For I cannot overcome
This trial on my own.
So give it to You I will, Lord.
Your faithfulness* You've shown

To me time and again.
Certainly, it's in the Book.
Help me to really focus
And have a good look.

At Your doing right,
Helping saints pull through.
Good is where You want me.
Good You'll lead me to.†

You may not choose
To give me full relief
And take it all away.

But You will sow
Treasures in my spirit
If with You I will stay.‡

So no matter how it looks
To my finite mind,
Help me to rest in faith
When answers I cannot find.**

Lord, let us all break out
Of spiritual confinement.
Make us who You want us to be.
Lord, do Your refinement.

----

* "Surely his salvation is near those who fear him, that his glory may dwell in our land. Love and faithfulness meet together; righteousness and peace kiss each other" (Ps. 85:9–10).

† "The Lord will indeed give what is good" (Ps. 85:12); "And we know that in all things God works for the good of those who love him, who have been called according to his purpose" (Rom. 8:28).

‡ "I am the vine; you are the branches. If you remain in me and I in you, you will bear much fruit; apart from me you can do nothing" (John 15:5).

** God is eternal; we are finite. We were never meant to fully grasp or fully understand Him or His Word because it is "God-breathed" (2 Tim. 3:16a). We need to accept and embrace our limitations when it comes to understanding the ways of God (Isa. 55:8–9).

See Me Through

We turn away and sin,
Deny Him access in.
And His heart does feel the pain

Of separation
From the destination
To be like Jesus through the rain.

The sting of sin
Produces a gap
Between me and a loving Savior.

But as I repent
And plead for
His mercy all the more,

He doesn't even blink
But accepts me right back,
Forgiving as He goes.

He's not like us,
For we hold on
To anger and to our woes.

What an awesome privilege
To call Jesus my Friend.

Please stay with me and see me through
Right to the very end.*

---

* "For this God is our God for ever and ever; he will be our guide even to the end" (Ps. 48:14).

ℒITTLE ℬIRDS

Little birds,
I see you fly.
I am envious of this.

To fly and waft
High in the heavens
Is my sincere wish.

Today I find myself flattened
By a trial so big and tough.
Causes me to wonder why
You have to make it so very rough.

But I know Your trials
Are there to test and try.
Could it really be true?
Even in this, I could fly?

You ask me to wait*
And hope in You.
Then You make me soar
Like an eagle, You do!

Even in the trial,
You give me Your joy.
It acts as a buffer,
It acts as a buoy.

So weave your web.
Lord, do your work.
And I'll stay right close to You,

For I know
In You are
Still the answers for true.

---

* "But those who wait on the LORD
shall renew their strength.
They shall mount up with wings like eagles;
they shall run and not grow weary,
they shall walk and not be faint" (Isa. 40:31 NKJV).

We were confined for weeks to the institution because of the SARS outbreak in April 2003. On the first day we were allowed out, I went to sit in the garden and wrote the following.

FREEDOM

When we think of freedom,
We think of things like this.
Walking on an open beach.
Lovemaking sealed with a kiss.

We think of horseback rides,
Playground slides,
Cars and bicycles too.

We don't think of wheelchairs
And their enemies, the stairs,
As being instruments of truth.

But there is a freedom
Of a spiritual kind
That brings hope and love anew.

It grows in our hearts
In the midst of
The profound suffering we do.

So please embrace
Your suffering for true.
Jesus is trying to make
You more like Him—yes, you.

---

* "To the Jews who had believed him, Jesus said, 'If you hold to my teaching you are really my disciples. Then you will know the truth, and the truth will set you free'" (John 8:31–32).

A PEARL

Though you feel heavy
And burdened with care,
And it's a long road
From here to there,

Here in the intensity
Of the grief you feel,
It's hard to believe you can
Be content* again for real.

But, "my yoke is easy
And my burden is light."†
He is the Master
At making us bright.

Bright stars for Him.
It's always what He hopes:
That you will take your trials
And do more than just cope.

Rejoice in suffering?‡
It seems absurd.
Seems like the craziest
Thing I've ever heard.

But rejoice we can,
And rejoice we will

If, through our trials,
We cleave to Him still.

If we but bring it to Him,
We can watch as He makes
A pearl from the common grain
Of sand that He takes.

---

* "I have learned to be content whatever the circumstances. I know what it is to be in need and I know what it is to have plenty. I have learned the secret of being content in any and every situation, whether well fed or hungry, whether living in plenty or in want. I can do all this through him who gives me strength" (Phil. 4:11b–13; written while Paul was in prison).

† "Come to me, all you who are weary and burdened, and I will give you rest. Take my yoke upon you and learn from me, for I am gentle and humble in heart, and you will find rest for your souls. For my yoke is easy and my burden is light" (Matt. 11:28–30).

‡ "[W]e ... rejoice in hope of the glory of God. And not only that, but we also glory in tribulations, knowing that tribulation produces perseverance; and perseverance, character; and character, hope" (Rom. 5:2b–4 NKJV); "[B]ut rejoice to the extent that you partake of Christ's sufferings, that when His glory is revealed, you may also be glad with exceeding joy" (1 Pet. 4:13 NKJV).

ALONE

"And when I am alone, give me Jesus."*

Such lilting and profound words
I feel are yet so true.
I find myself alone.
Jesus, it's just me and You.

Betrayed by people
I thought I could count on.
My problem then a hill,
Now a mountain.

Oh, trouble,
Why have you
Come on so very strong?

I looked for
Human support.
Or could I have been wrong?

To draw me closer is why
You've allowed them all to go away.
So I'll lean all the more
On You, dear Lord, today.

---

* From "Give Me Jesus," sung by Fernando Ortega.

Keeping Up

Dear Lord:

I find it hard
Just keeping up.
Keeping in step with You
I really find hard to do.

For time barrels on,
So much to do.
Can hardly find time
For me and for You.

My quiet time, it seems,
Is the first to get
Squeezed out of my day.
Oh, Lord, please help me

Discipline myself and
Let You have Your way,
Your way with me.
You long for me to be close

And develop spiritual intimacy.
As Fernando Ortega sings,
"Don't let me
Come home a stranger." Amen.

A SPIRITUAL WEIGHTLIFTER

Every day,
Troubles.

Troubles come.
It's His way
Every day.

I get so tired,
I get so frustrated.
When I think I've had enough,
You heap on more.

But help me to understand
That Your ways are not mine.*
Help me go to You
Time after time after time.

And help me to accept
Your divine help when You give it,
So the horror of my sin
I don't have to relive it.

Help me† be
A spiritual weightlifter
So I can, in turn, be for others

An emotional hatelifter.

---

* "'For my thoughts are not your thoughts, neither are your ways my ways,' declares the Lord" (Isa.55:8).

† Prolific author and speaker Joyce Meyer says that sometimes we just need to repeat, "Lord, help me! Help me! Help me!"

TURN AND TRUST

Turn and trust
The Savior true,
For He really wants
You—yes, you.

You need to acknowledge
This problem called sin.
You need to say yes
And let His love in.

For sin erects walls
Between you and He.
Spiritual wholeness
Is what we need.

He paid the price,
He paid it in full—
The penalty for your sin and mine.

And He does forgive
No matter what,
Time after time after time.

He stands at the door and knocks
With arms outstretched and open wide.
He longs to empower you with His love.
He offers Himself in this life as the Guide.

Just say, "Jesus, come in.
Be the Lord of my soul.
Forgive all of my sins, and
Make serving You my true goal."

For being holy,
He cannot abide
By the sin in your heart
That you try to hide.

So give it to Him.
Give Him your life too.
'Cause He freely gave His
For me and for you.

Do it now, my friend.
You know you really must.
To be right with a holy God,
You need to but turn and trust.

DEATH DEW

Every day,
So hard
To push it away.

Death dew
Collects
Each day anew.

A fresh layer descends
On me this very day.
Can't help but wish
That it would just have its way.

Ready to go and find relief
From the endless barrage of pain.
Cried so many tears of grief,
It seems again and again and again.

Tired of the struggle
And of the fight too.
Rather wish sweet death
Would embrace me, would do …

… do its work,
For I've made my peace
With my Savior.
Now I seek relief.

But wait—You are doing a work.
You are helping me see
It's all about You
And not about me.

You want to bring
Glory through the pain,*
Draw others, and me, to You.

As folks reach out to me
In my grief, they find themselves,
Discovering You for true.†

So please help me, Lord,
Temptations to suicide to shun.**
For I will wait for Your time.
Not my will, but Yours be done.‡

---

* My prayer when I wrote this poem (can you make it yours?): "I want to know Christ—yes, to know the power of his resurrection and participation in his sufferings, becoming like him in his death, and so, somehow, attaining to the resurrection from the dead" (Phil. 3:10–11); Also: "Dear friends, do not be surprised at the fiery ordeal that has come on you to test you, as though something strange were happening to you. But rejoice inasmuch as you participate in the sufferings of Christ, so that you may be overjoyed when his glory is revealed" (1 Pet. 4:12–13).

† "Truly I tell you, whatever you did for one of the least of these brothers or sisters of mine, you did for me" (Matt. 25:40).

**When I wrote this, I was new to the wheelchair.

‡ Jesus in His Garden of Gethsemane: "Going a little farther, he fell with his face to the ground and prayed, 'My Father, if it is possible, may this cup be taken from me. Yet not as I will, but as you will'" (Matt. 26:39). With these words, He took on more than we will ever be asked to do, regardless of the trouble we face. He took on all sin past, present, and future—not just the agony of the cross. Can we bear our cross with the same patience, dignity, and grace Jesus showed for us as an example?

For this God is our God forever and ever;
he will be our guide even to the end.
—Psalm 48:14

Printed in the United States
By Bookmasters